Off the Shelf

How to run a successful primary school library and promote reading

Lucy Bakewell
The School Librarian of the Year

Off the Shelf

© 2010 Lucy Bakewell and Carel Press

Published by Carel Press Ltd
4 Hewson St
Carlisle CA2 5AU
Tel + 44 1228 538928
Fax + 44 1228 591816
info@carelpress.co.uk
www.carelpress.co.uk
email the author: lucy@carelpress.co.uk

Editorial, design and web team: Jack Gregory, Chas White
Readers: Nikki Heath, Sally Duncan, Chris Shepherd, Debbie Maxwell, Ann Batey, Stephen White
Cover design: Anne Louise Kershaw
Back cover photos: Summer Reading Challenge, the Reading Agency. Photographer: Dave Warren

Printed by: Interpress, Budapest

CIP Data: British Library Cataloguing in Publication Data is available

ISBN: 978 1 905600 22 9

Off the Shelf – online access
When you buy this book you also get online access to the copiable resources and templates.
This is for
• ease of printing
• access to full colour
• use on a whiteboard

You will also find a copy of the Useful Websites list (page 23) online, with live links.
Email us to obtain your code to access these resources: office@carelpress.co.uk

Age note:
Key Stage 1 (KS1): age 5-7
Key Stage 2 (KS2): age 7-11

See all our library resources (copiable books, posters, digital resources) at www.carelpress.co.uk

Lucy Bakewell

The School Library Association School Librarian of the Year

Lucy Bakewell won the School Librarian of the Year award in October 2009. Lucy is the librarian of Hill West Primary School in Sutton Coldfield and the first primary school librarian to win this coveted award from the School Library Association. The judging panel had visited many outstanding school libraries in order to draw up the shortlist for the award.

Ginette Doyle, Chair of the judging panel, said: 'Primary schools are vital in inspiring children to read and reading is so important in the development of children, expanding their imagination, their knowledge, their vocabulary. They are also the places where children begin to learn to learn, where information skills are first taught, creating individuals competent in finding information. Few primary schools can afford to have a librarian and many rely on dedicated individuals, such as Lucy, to run their libraries. Lucy inspires her pupils to love books and reading and she inspires the adults around her. Hill West School is an example of a marvellous school where reading and books are central to learning, much of which is down to Lucy. We feel that it is really important to raise the profile of good primary school library practice, to demonstrate that with the right person in place wonderful things can be achieved.'

In accepting the award Lucy said: 'I am ecstatic and honoured to be given this award for something I love doing. I have the best job in the world and it's a joy to spend time in the library. I feel passionate about making the library a space that children feel is their own and am delighted to receive the honour for the children and for the school. It is exceptionally important that a primary school has won for the first time. It is vital to enthuse and engage children in books and reading from an early age.'

For more information about the award see the School Library Association website www.sla.org.uk

CONTENTS

Copiable Resources & Templates

At the back of this book is a collection of templates for copying, but as a buyer of this book you also get access to the resources and templates online for:

• ease of printing in full colour
• use on a whiteboard
• live website links on the Useful Websites list

Page references are shown in brackets next to the titles.

You can download these resources in full colour from www.carelpress.co.uk/offtheshelf
Email office@carelpress.co.uk for your username and password to access these resources:

Username: Password:

INTRODUCTION

When I first took on the job as School Librarian, it crossed my mind that I may have bitten off more than I could chew. Had I any clue what I had let myself in for? Having had no previous experience and, only armed with a passion for books and reading, I blindly began a journey that has been both challenging and an utter joy.

I believe with the right pointers and advice every school can have, and should have, an inspiring school library. Whether you are a full time manager, librarian, teacher, teaching assistant (like me) or parent, our job is not to create the 'perfect' library, but to create the perfect library for our school's individual needs. To do this we have to wear many hats: teacher, information specialist, administrator, promoter, advisor and, most importantly, inspirer.

We change lives by supporting learning and teaching in our schools. It is crucial to inspire children at a young age and make them passionate about reading; expanding their imagination, knowledge and their vocabulary.

The Librarian's knowledge and enthusiasm for books puts her or him in a unique position to influence all the children. The librarian can promote reading throughout the school; bringing stories to life through many different means: themed events, author visits, reading initiatives and book awards to name but a few.

I was once a reluctant reader myself, so I understand the influence reading can have on learning. By the age of eleven I had never read a book, which, of course, affected my literacy skills. I then read Rebecca's World by Terry Nation. This was the catalyst I needed. I read it from cover to cover and was transported to another world. I was hooked! Just one book opened a gateway that has never been closed.

It was my mother who bought me that book, the one person in my life who always surrounded me with stories; from books, from her own imagination and her own life. With such support at home, what was it that stopped me from picking up a book and reading it? I always wonder; had there been a great Library for me to access at school, would my experience have been different?

It is the School Librarian's job to create an environment that not only belongs to the children but also impacts on the whole school and reaches out to those beyond the school walls. We need to create a reading ethos for pupils, staff, management and parents; giving the children a truly rounded support network for their reading.

On being asked to write this book I was very excited about the opportunity to create something specifically tailored for Primary Schools. Then I sat down and tried to imagine the kind of handbook I would have liked to guide me. I remember, three years ago, searching through the internet trying to find such a book. Although there are some titles, none really captured the Librarian's role or resources required in a Primary school.

I know only too well the host of challenges we face everyday: lack of space, budget, support, time and experience to name but a few. But it is also these constraints that have helped me be more creative, to think 'Off the Shelf' and find ways to create a great library despite them.

What makes everything worthwhile is when that one child discovers the joy of reading from a book you've recommended, or a parent is inspired to read to their child from an event you've organised.

I hope in this book I have managed to combine all the key elements and put together a handbook to help you create the inspiring Library your children deserve.

Lucy Bakewell

THE WOW FACTOR

'A display has more impact than almost anything else you can do in the library!'

One of the quickest, most effective and value for money ways to make your library look inviting and lively is by using displays. From the smallest corner to the largest space, there is always a wall, window, ceiling or cupboard top for a display. The longer I do this job the more creative I have become using every space available for displays.

I truly believe that the library belongs to the children who use it and the library's appearance should make this obvious. Displays are one of the most effective ways of achieving this.

Here are some of my favourite display ideas; from the very quick to those which require a little more time and effort. Hopefully you will find some that suit you, your time and budget.

Make an instant impact with these essentials

Dewey system: When you first set up a school library there are one or two essential displays. The main one is a clear outline of the Dewey system.

Print out a template from the website (there is a choice) or photocopy my version from p47. Laminate it and display wherever you have space. You could even hang it from the ceiling if space is tight.

If you make your own it is obviously up to you to decide how detailed you want to make it. I have always found that at Primary level the simpler and more visual it is the better.

Colour Coding: If you have inherited a library that isn't arranged by the Dewey system then you can create your own organisation system that suits your books and the school. Simple colour coding with coloured labels on the book spines and a poster explaining what the colours mean will quickly make a difference. Even if you use Dewey, you might colour code some books. Many high schools and public libraries do this for their fiction. It's popular with children because it's easy to understand. You will find a version of the template on the website with boxes for colour coding.

Notes and tips

My inspiration for all my displays is watching the reactions on the children's faces the first time they see them.
If I get a smile or a gasp then my job has been worthwhile

How to find your books!

004	ICT
200s	Religion
300s	People, Society
500-549	Science
550-599	Nature
600s	Technology
700s	Art, Music, Sport
800s	Poems
900s	Geography, History

The How to find your books template (p47) shows areas of the Dewey system as I use them. You can download other versions from the website

DEWEY ADVICE
If you are uncertain about how to set up or use the Dewey system, the first point of contact should be your local School Library Service

Notes and tips

Library noticeboard with pupil librarians

Project loans:
School library Services provide project loans of books, posters and other resources. Some even loan objects eg a collection on themes ranging from the Second World War to world religions.

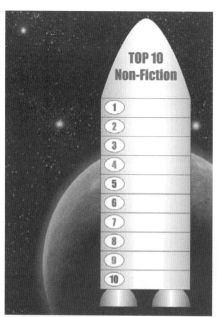

Above: Copiable template for Non-fiction Top 10 Rocket, see page 55 or download in colour from the website.

Library Noticeboard: This is a vital display and the main way of promoting events and giving information about the library to the rest of the school. Size doesn't matter as long as it is big enough to see when you come into the library and it can fit relevant information on as well as the names and photos of any pupil librarians you may have. I have found my librarians always get a kick out of having their pictures on display. I always like to give things a theme and use a front cover of a book as the photo frame. *See Pupil Librarian photo frames template, p48.*

The next stage, if you've time and a budget

When you have more time and space try these display ideas. They not only brighten up the library but also involve the children in their library.

Pupil Owned Dewey Display: This is an idea I picked up from a library in Italy and one that gives the children total ownership of the system in a child friendly, visual way.

1 Cut up a pile of white card into squares or rectangles (size is up to you).

2 On a piece of card draw a box and colour it for one of the main Dewey sections. Below add the section number e.g. an orange box labelled 700s.

3 Decide on the main three or four topics covered by the subject e.g. sport, music, art, films (you will need a piece of card for each topic).

4 Give the children a piece of card and ask them to draw a picture that represents the topic area.

5 Repeat for each Dewey section.

This idea can either be displayed on a wall or, as I have done, use a pocketed photo display hanging to place the cards in. These can be purchased from DIY or home stores.

A library plan is a great way of directing children to the right place to look.

Top Tens (they do exactly what they say on the tin)

My three main categories are most popular non-fiction titles, fiction titles and authors, but you could change them to suit your needs and resources. If you have a computerised management system, you will find reports on the system that will give you this information instantly. If you haven't, then you can soon create top tens that you can research manually.

It's nice to theme each top ten display to make them fun and visual; I use a sunflower for fiction, a rocket for non-fiction, and a chart style run down for authors (see templates p55-57). These are just ideas; feel free to let your imagination run wild!

Be ambitious! Time and money to spend!

If time and space are not an issue, why not try to make your displays even more interactive.

Display of Recommended Websites

There is no doubt that the internet is a huge source of information and a massive influence on children today. Rather than fight it the modern school library should not only embrace it but promote its safe use for research into books and authors on the web. Most popular authors have their own websites and there are many that include book reviews, games, poetry and more.

This information can be displayed either in the library or in the ICT area of the school, creating a link between the two. You don't just have to promote reading in the library!

For more impact, use our Books on the Web template (p52) or you could display the web addresses around a picture of a computer.

Top Readers

This is a great way to encourage reading and the children always look forward to the end of every half term when I hand out the certificates (template p49) for the top readers in assembly.

If you have a computerised management system, information on each child's reading history is readily available. If not then you could keep a manual tally of how many books each child has borrowed.

Every half term I pick up to three children from each year group who have borrowed the most books. As well as receiving certificates, their names are displayed on our Top Reader board (template p53) in the library. I use stars (template p54) to display their names, but you could use whatever you want. This is a simple display that has a huge impact throughout the school.

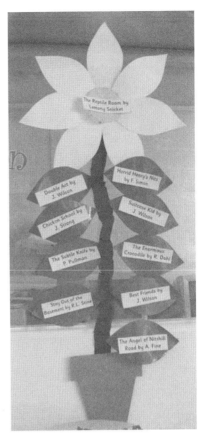

Above: Fiction Top 10 flower I made for the Hill West library (template on p56 and on the website in colour and larger sizes.)

Above: My Top Readers display.
Below: Copiable template for Top Readers display – see templates on pages 53 and 54, or download from the website.

Successful Library
Displays (Carel Press)
by Fran Knight &
Pat Pledger

If you don't have any
fabric, then paper or
plastic table cloths that
can be bought from
supermarkets or discount
stores can be just as
effective.

THEMED DISPLAYS

Throughout the school year there are a host of book events and celebration days (see Calendar of Key Events p24-25). Use these events to theme not only your displays but the whole library. Here are a few ideas to create a real wow factor. Just choose a theme and away you go.

Make an instant impact, with these essentials

Book displays can be a simple way to liven up a small corner, shelf top or ceiling using hangings (see accessorising p12). They can be changed and updated on a regular basis to keep things interesting or why not really go to town when you have a special theme in the library like Halloween.

The first thing to do is pick your theme. This could be as simple as a genre of writing e.g. horror or a specific topic area such as poetry. If you are working on a flat surface place a colourful or themed drape for a covering.

Choose a selection of books, both non-fiction and fiction if appropriate, and arrange the books on the covered surface. You can use book stands, but they are not necessary as books can be displayed standing up or lying down. To make the display even more interesting, place small boxes under the drape so books can be displayed at different heights.

If your display has a theme, collect props that complement it and arrange them amongst the books or try a centre piece e.g. a nativity tableau at Christmas or cauldron at Halloween, it will really bring it to life!

The next stage, if you've time and a budget

Library Display Board in the school entrance

To create a reading ethos around the whole school, ask for a prominent display board, where you can promote events or library themes to the wider school community. The best place would be in the entrance hall where it can also be seen by parents and visitors.

This is your chance to create an inspirational display that entices the children to visit the library and encourages a love of reading. Try to change the display every half term so it is always fresh and new. If done well it can create a real buzz around school, with the children looking forward to it changing. Ideas for themes:

- Match it to a theme in the library

- Promote an upcoming event; one at school, in the library or a literary event e.g. World Book Day (see Calendar of Key Events p24-25)

- Link it to a new film, or TV programme, that is based on a book (most films are based on books).

- Promote a love of reading using inspirational quotes or posters

- Book reviews

Be ambitious! Time and money to spend!

For the ultimate way to give your library the wow factor why not theme and decorate the whole library to mark special events? But don't worry, it doesn't mean you have to blow the budget. All you need is a bit of creativity and an eye for a bargain.

As discussed in Book Displays, always keep your eye out for props, banners, decorations etc that you can use to theme and decorate the library. The easiest way to theme the whole library is to focus on big annual celebrations e.g. Christmas, Easter, Halloween, Valentine's Day, but you could also use events like Roald Dahl Day and make banners and props yourself. If you have a window in the library, dress it with pictures.

Notes and tips

'Our library is WICKED! It's bright and colourful and kids love to come here' Alfie, Year 6

BUDGET STRETCHER
I don't advocate blowing your budget on props. Be creative, think off the shelf! This year I found Christmas bottle boxes in the shapes of snowmen and reindeers in a local shop for a £1! Always be on the look out for props during the year. Discount stores are a great source of inspiration, particularly after the event. It's amazing the bargains you can pick up when Halloween or Easter is over!

Return your books here

Above: Return your books here – a copiable template to use near your Returns Box. See p62 or download from the website

ACCESSORISING

Once you have your shelves, books and displays the next thing you need to think about is accessorising your space. I truly believe that a library has to be child friendly; an extension of their bedroom where they feel safe, secure and comfortable. As librarians we have to create an environment and atmosphere that inspires reading. This can be achieved by using accessories that appeal to a child.

Like everything in this chapter you can accessorise according to the time, space and budget you have. When the budget is tight, which unfortunately it is most of the time, always have a look in the many discount stores on the high street. If your budget is a little more healthy go straight to the DIY/home stores. However, if your budget will allow you a little more luxury then buy some wow accessories from Library outfitters. Even the smallest of rugs or cushions can make a huge difference and instantly change the feel of your space.

Basic Accessories

Returns and Suggestion Boxes: There are two basic essentials to have in the library: a Returns Box and a Suggestions Box. Don't just use plain boxes; make a feature of them by using a child friendly, non traditional container to do the same job. Think about all the funky storage ideas there are for children's bedrooms! Remember it is their space and every accessory should reflect that.

I was really lucky to find a pet sleeping box that is shaped like a cat (with a tail and ears). It's bright, fun and does a great job as a Returns Box. It wasn't expensive and the children love him so much that they have even named him Spike! In the same home store I discovered a pelican head that has a beak which lifts up to reveal a storage space in its mouth. My Year 6 librarians thought it would make a great Suggestion Box and they even cut up bits of paper in the shape of fish, so the children can feed him their ideas.

Mid Range Accessories

Hangings: I have always loved hanging things from the ceiling in the classroom; from children's work to maths, vocabulary to art. It really breaks up a space and can instantly make an area more interactive. So whether space is an issue or not, hangings can be a very visual way to display books in your library.

How about using a hanging clothes drier? They can be picked up cheaply from most discount stores and the pegs are a great way to display several books at a time. I have even decorated them with tinsel for Christmas, they look a little like an advent crown!

If you want to add a splash of colour, many home stores sell mesh or net hanging storage in primary colours. They are designed to hold toys, but books sit inside them just as well. You may want to mix them with cuddly toys to give it a more child friendly theme.

Reading corner: To inspire children to interact with books, we have to give them the opportunity to do just that. As in any classroom, the reading corner is a quiet area, where the children can tuck themselves away to quietly read or where a group can share a book together.

If you have a little space in your library, then create a quiet reading area for children. An easy way to do this is by using simple scatter cushions. These don't have to be expensive, just comfy and bright.

At a local home store, I found some small circles of colourful carpet. I only bought a few to scatter around the floor, but the children love to make patterns with them and sit on them to read.

If your budget will allow, most library furniture companies have some amazing cushions, small carpet tiles or colourful rugs which can really make a reading corner come to life.

Designer Accessories

Seating area: For those of you lucky enough to have a designated room for your library, why not create a seating area for individual/group reading, research or work. Whether you have a table and chairs, settee style seating or benches, a seating area is a brilliant way to encourage the children to spend quality time in the library.

Library furniture suppliers have amazing products available in a range of colours, styles and prices. Before committing any of your budget to these make sure you research exactly what you want your seating area to be used for. If it's for reading, look for designs that create a group environment like circular seats. If it's for work then choose something that can be used by several children at once. Whatever you choose, always try to use your space to the best effect, make it colourful and most importantly child friendly.

See this website
For more ideas and inspiration see the photos of school library displays at carelpress.co.uk/libraryresources/ Displayphotos

Above: Borrow a book today! – a copiable template to use anywhere in your library. See p61 or download from the website

Carpet from a library supplier

Make a big effort to involve children, teachers and parents in making your displays. They will look better and it will be more fun for everyone!

ENGAGING PUPILS IN READING

The Library is a fantastic resource in any school and, if effective, will help children to engage in reading. But how do we get the children to engage in the Library?

'The surprise on children's faces when they discover a book they suggested on the shelves is priceless!'

Pupil Ownership

As discussed in the last chapter, the Library belongs to the pupils and I have found that the best way to get the children to interact with the Library is to give them not only ownership of the Library design, but also ownership in how it is run and the choice of books stocked there.

Book selection

Buying the right selection of books for the Library is vital to its success. There are so many titles to choose from; it can be a minefield. I remember my first visit to Peters Booksellers in Birmingham. I stood there looking at the never ending book shelves, filled with every genre of book you can imagine and wondered where to start. Without reading all the books available, how did I begin to know which books the children wanted to read or which were the best ones for them to read? With a limited budget, I had to get it right. The only way I have found to do this is to be as organised as possible. Use all the tools you have to put together a wish list and stick to it.

Above: Tell me what you want to read: a copiable poster for you to use with your Suggestion Box. See p60 or download from the website

Make an instant impact with these essentials

Suggestion Box: It has been said many times that children are our best critics. They are very discerning and certainly know their own minds when it comes to things they like and dislike. Books are no exception.

The simplest way I have found to buy the books the children want to read is to ask them. Giving them a voice really makes them feel valued and a part of the Library. Placing a Suggestion Box in the Library allows the children to suggest books that they have already read and feel others would like to read or books that they would like to read that are not already in the Library. I always suggest to teachers that they use some of their class time in the Library to allow the children to discuss book choices and write suggestions; teachers tell me it prompts great class discussion and gives them a good insight into pupils' reading behaviour.

I sometimes think the children don't believe that I actually do read their suggestions. The surprise on their faces when they discover a book they suggested on the shelves – it's priceless!

The next stage, if you've time and a budget

I think we are all quite aware that budgets are tight and we can't always buy the selection of books that we, or the children, would like to. I heard about this idea from another school and it seemed to work so well that I decided to give it a go myself. Not only does it give the children a chance to get involved in book selection, but it can also be extended into a day event.

We decided to have a fund raising day for the library, the difference being we did not ask the children to raise money, we asked them to raise books. We chose to hold our event during Book Week, but it could be any day of the year. We sent out flyers inviting the children to come to school that day dressed as their favourite book character.

Normally at such events we would ask the children to bring in 50p, but this time we asked the children if they would donate a book from home that they had read and would recommend to someone else. By donating the book to the library they were allowing another child in the school the opportunity to read that book under their recommendation. The children loved the idea of being able to share their books and stories with others and it really inspired them. We have never had such a huge response to an event before and so many great books were donated. The crucial thing was that these were children's books which had been recommended by children.

PUPIL LIBRARIANS

A great way to get the children involved in the running of the Library is by creating Librarian jobs. You will amazed at how keen the children are to get involved in the running of the library, from simple tasks like issuing books to creating displays and managing stock. Their help can also take some of the strain off you too!

Make an instant impact with these essentials

Class Librarians: A quick and simple way to get pupils from Reception to Year 6 involved in running the Library is by creating Class Librarians. It is up to the teachers, but we find it works best to give two children from each class the job and rotate them every term or half term. Their primary responsibility is to issue and return books during class library sessions, but you can add to their roles as you or the class teacher sees fit.

The next stage, if you've time and a budget

Year 6 Librarians: It doesn't matter how large or small your library space is, keeping it tidy is a continual and time consuming job. We are always looking for ways to make our lives easier, look no further than Year 6!

> A Year 4 child once told me, "Mrs. Bakewell the book I've been wanting to read for ages is now in the Library. How did you know?" He had obviously forgotten he had suggested it only 2 weeks before!

It amazes and delights me every September how many children put their names forward to be Year 6 Librarians. Since introducing them four years ago, their role has developed each year.

> They really enjoy putting books back on the shelves and sometimes have competitions to see who can find the shelves the fastest or with their eyes closed. They challenged me to that one and no one has beaten me yet!

Every September the school advertises jobs for Year 6 pupils; one of which is as a Librarian. Pupils who are interested put their names forward to their teachers. I look through the list with the teachers and choose 6 pupils we feel are most suitable. I always like to choose a mixture of boys and girls from the list; children who are high level readers, children who love books but struggle with their reading and reluctant readers, although they all need to be reliable and enthusiastic! I really want the job to make an impact on the children and help them to enjoy reading by working with books.

In the beginning, their job solely entailed them coming to the Library for half an hour at lunchtime twice a week. During that half an hour, they generally tidied the shelves as well as putting returned books away. The great thing about this simple task is that they have to learn the Dewey system well in order to put the books back on the shelves correctly.

Be ambitious! Time and money to spend!

"I wanted to be a Librarian to learn more about books and how the Library works"

This was the statement, from one of my Librarians, that made me reassess their role and ultimately extend their responsibilities in the Library.

Over the year, I found that the more time they spent in the Library, the more they wanted to know and the more questions they asked. Children are intrigued to know how a library is run, from the management system to how and why books are Dewey numbered. Why not use this curiosity to develop their skills further? Here are a few of the jobs you can delegate:

- Using a Subject Index to allocate Dewey numbers to new books according to their subject

- Printing Dewey labels on the label machine (one of their favourite toys!)

- Sticking Dewey numbers and stickers onto books

- Placing bar codes in all the new books

They really got a kick out of seeing how a book gets from the box to the shelf and it taught them invaluable library skills. I was lucky enough to catch up with one of my former Librarians and she told me that she has become a Librarian at her Secondary School partly because the Librarian was so impressed with her knowledge and Library skills.

As discussed previously, I try to choose a variety of children to become Year 6 Librarians. However, it is important that they are all keen, reliable and hard working. If you have Librarians with all these skills you can utilise them even further within school.

READING MENTORS

Reading mentors are a great resource within a school. They help develop reading skills and confidence in younger pupils being mentored, as well as giving the mentor, whether a reluctant or prolific reader, a sense of achievement and self confidence that is priceless.

When I first approached my Librarians about becoming mentors, they were a little hesitant, but after discussing it with them they decided that they would like to start by reading with Reception children, so they could practise and gain confidence.

We set it up like this: mentors would visit Reception once a week and be given a reading buddy, chosen by Reception staff. The mentors would spend 15 minutes with their buddy reading and talking to them about a story chosen by the teacher. As the mentors gained confidence and began to get to know the child they would choose books they felt the child would enjoy and were within their own reading capability. It's up to you how long the mentoring of one child continues, we found it useful to change the buddy every term, that way up to 18 children can be mentored. The system works well, particularly with boys, who really enjoyed sharing books with older boys, looking up to them as role models.

**Where to find
your books**

**Primary Library
Find It Index**

Your school name here

CAREL

Where to find your books is an editable guide to library subjects and classification numbers for primary schools. It comes as an Excel file which you can edit and print, with a specially designed cover with your school name on – see above. Available from www.carelpress.co.uk

RELUCTANT READERS

"A reluctant reader is a child who has not been given the right book YET."

I heard this at a seminar by Alec Williams (consultant and former chair of the School Library Association) and found it such a profound statement that I have never forgotten it. For the majority of children reading is a skill that needs little encouragement, but for others, and I think we can all name a few, reading is not the enjoyable experience we promote.

The aim of an effective school library is to encourage all children to read, however, we know that this can be harder to achieve with some children than others. Research shows that the majority of reluctant readers are boys.

I was one of the few girls who was a reluctant reader. I didn't read my first book until I was 11. For me reading was a chore and, as a tomboy, there were no books out there that inspired me to pick up a book and read. Luckily for me, my mum spent the time talking to me about books, what

'I really enjoy being a reading mentor to younger children, it helped me to become more confident with my own reading.'

interested me and what I looked for in a good book. From that she researched titles until she found a book she thought I would like. The book was Rebecca's World: Journey to the Forbidden Planet by Terry Nation. As a big Doctor Who fan, the thought of reading a book by the creator of the Daleks was enough to make me pick up the book and read it. The more I read, the more I enjoyed it, so I read on. I had found the right book and never looked back. But for many children there is not the opportunity to find the 'right' book and most teachers do not have the time in the school day. As Librarians we are in a unique position to bridge this gap.

BOYS INTO BOOKS

As already discussed, we all have a responsibility to ensure that young people are introduced to the world of books as early in life as possible. If not, we not only hinder their progress academically, but also deprive them of a precious source of intellectual and emotional stimulation which can be enjoyed anywhere, at any time, and either alone or with others. While many children have already discovered the joys of reading for pleasure, sadly a large number, particularly boys, remain to be convinced. It is an unfortunate fact that boys in particular are reluctant readers. Research has shown that by the time boys get to secondary school many are already two levels behind in their reading age. There are some great initiatives available to encourage boys to read. In 2007 the School Library Association produced a new list of books targeted specifically at teenage boys. The books on the list were made available, through DCSF funding, not only to secondary schools but also to Pupil Referral Units, thus reaching those young people excluded from mainstream education. And while the books were selected for their particular appeal to boys, they have also proved very popular with girls.

In 2008 the DCSF in partnership with the School Library Association decided to focus on nurturing the enjoyment of reading at a much earlier age and introduced their Riveting Reads booklist, aimed at boys in primary schools. *Boys into Books 5 to 11* made available to schools a huge variety of books, including old and new classics and alternative genres of writing such as graphic novels. The list also included guidance for those wishing to introduce the books.

The aim of the initiative was to arm schools with the resources to target boys and, through great resources, inspire them to read.

When I received my first box of books, I was a little stumped about what to do with them. The first thing I decided was to make a special area in the library where these books would be displayed. But who would borrow them?

It was then that my Head and I sat down to discuss how to really make the most of these great, free books! We decided that we should target reluctant readers from certain year groups (we chose years 3 and 4 initially). We would create a reading group which would meet once a week to read and chat together, and to create a buzz, would be allowed the privilege of choosing from their own collection of books.

We began the reading group the next term and have continued and expanded it to other year groups since then.

Even if you did not have access to the free book box, you can still create your own version. Just gather together some books of high interest to boys (a wide selection of reading levels to appeal to different year groups) and create your own Boys Into Books section in the library. This may be a whole shelf or just the top of a cupboard, it doesn't really matter, the main thing is to decorate it and make it look special. Alternatively, buy a large plastic box with a lid (a cheap one from the high street will do), then decorate it and fill it with books. The main objective of Boys Into Books is to make the boys' area special and exclusive, somewhere that is just for them. Then choose your target group and away you go!

I love this initiative as it gives me a chance to really get to know the boys and how they make book choices. Not only does it give me the opportunity to group read with them, but it enables you to guide them in their reading for understanding. However, my favourite aspect is the discussion time. As teaching staff we rarely have enough time in the timetable to sit down and talk to the children about what they want to read. I always find it fascinating when talking to the boys to discover what really excites them in a book. A great example was one boy who was a real cool dude; into break dancing, rapping, fashion and so on. Everyone had presumed he wanted to read more modern stories about football and spies. However, during our discussions in the first session he told me that the stories he really wanted to read were about good and evil, magic, mythical creatures and heroes, subjects quite unlike what we had presumed he would be interested in. From there he began to read the Beast Quest series by Adam Blade; books with all the ingredients that interested him. From that point he has never looked back, he had found the book to begin his lifelong journey of reading.

If you have any spare time in your week, please give these sessions a go. As librarians we are passionate about inspiring children to read and these sessions really tick that box. To find out more information about Boys Into Books or just to get some inspiration from the Riveting Reads booklist they collated, see www.sla.org.uk.

Don't forget, these groups don't just have to be for boys. I can't tell you the number of times the girls have complained to me that it's not fair the boys get a special area and special books. One girl (who is an exceptionally good reader) said to me recently, "Mrs Bakewell, if I start reading badly, can I come to your group?" I quickly told her that this was not a good idea and that she would miss reading Jane Eyre!

> Decide how you want to run the sessions. If you don't have a lot of time, then as a trial choose one year group, maybe the year you work in. If you have more time then you could have a group of boys from several year groups and run more sessions during the week.

Template for an invitation to a Boys into Books club. See p50 or download from the website

Session Plans

Before the first session

The first thing to do is to create a specific area or shelf in the Library, where you can place high interest books for boys. I placed it in an area by the Reference section, little visited by the children. I decorated the area with a banner with Boys into Books on it. At the end of each reading session the boys are able to choose a book from the selection to take home and read.

Set the day and time of your session and send each boy an invitation (see template p50). They always love this as it makes them feel special and creates a buzz about the session.

Session 1:

This is really a getting to know you session and a chance to explain to the boys what you are going to do.

Introduction

Explain to the boys that they will be coming to the Library with you every week at the same time to read together and that they will be able to choose a book from their own special selection to take home and read.

Discussion

Ask the boys what they look for in a good book, do they look at the front cover, read the blurb, the opening page and so on? Discuss their answers and try to come to a consensus about how to choose a good book.

Then talk to them about what sort of books they would like to read; subjects, genres etc. Try to be specific to individuals so you can assess what books you can direct them to at the end of the session.

Main activity

Tell the boys that today they are going to make a special bookmark to use in their Boys into Books book (see template p51). They can design it themselves, using pictures of book characters they like; if they are struggling for ideas, let them look around the library for front covers they like and copy characters from there. When they have finished you can laminate them.

Plenary

Explain to the boys that next session they will be group reading with you. Introduce the book you will be reading and discuss the front cover and make predictions about what they think the story will be about.

Bookmark Template See p51 or download from the website

Finally allow the boys, with guidance from you, to choose a book from the Boys Into Books selection that fits the preference they discussed earlier. If they are unsure then ask them to try a book that you recommend. Tell them that you have not read this one and would value their opinion on it.

Session 2:

Introduction
Ask each child to give a brief book review of the book they took home last week. Discuss what they liked/didn't like about the book and whether they would like to try another book similar/different from the last one.

Main Activity
Remind the children about the book you introduced last week. Tell them that you are going to be reading this book together over the next few weeks. Begin reading the book, taking it in turns for each boy to read a page at a time out loud. As you read, stop occasionally to check understanding, to point out important parts or to predict what will happen next.

At the end of the chapter, or section, get the boys to recount what has happened and what they think will happen next.

Plenary
Give the boys an opportunity to change their book.

Each session from thereafter will take the same format until you finish the book. Remember to talk to the boys and teachers to keep a track as to the effect the sessions are having on their reading.

Continue the sessions until you decide that you want to change the group and give other boys an opportunity.

USING TECHNOLOGY

Soon all children should have access to a learning platform on the internet. Using this platform is a great way of engaging the children in reading whilst supporting their writing skills.

I am lucky enough to use a great library management system, Junior Librarian.net, which we have linked into our learning platform. It enables the children to access the Library database from home and search for books they would like to read, research authors they like and connects them to child-safe websites that may interest them according to their searches. This is all done in a truly engaging, colourful and child friendly environment, the children really enjoy using it and do not see it as a learning tool, merely a fun and exciting way to interact with their library.

However, my favourite toy on the system is the book review section. This allows the children to write book reviews of the books they have read from the library. These book reviews are then stored on the system so when a child does a search on a book they can read other children's reviews to help them make choices. This was so successful that we have introduced this as a termly literacy homework for all children. The children really enjoy contributing to the library and love reading other children's reviews; they are more likely to take advice from their peers than an adult!

Book Review Template. See p64 or download from the website

Don't worry if you haven't got a computerised management system - you'll have more money for books!

If you don't have a management system with this capability, you could easily set up your own system for children to write book reviews which you can then display.

The paper route

Draw up a template for a book review, simple for KS1 and more complex for lower and upper KS2 or use the template on p64. Ask teachers if they could set a book review as homework on a half termly/termly basis. Collect all the reviews and make an alphabetical book that can be displayed in the library. Children can then use it to help them choose books.

The computer route

If you have a learning platform set up at school, ask your ICT technician to set up a section for book reviews. Design a template on the computer and set up a book review homework as above. Then print off or save all the reviews and create a file that the children can access and use.

If you have the same management system as me or a similar one with a book review capability, try setting up a similar system to mine.

USEFUL WEBSITES

BBC Bitesize www.bbc.co.uk/schools/revision
BBC Cbeebies www.bbc.co.uk/cbeebies
CBBC www.bbc.co.uk/cbbc
Blue Peter www.bbc.co.uk/cbbc/bluepeter
Blue Peter Book Club
www.bbc.co.uk/cbbc/bluepeter/getinvolved/bookclub
Book Adventure www.bookadventure.org
Book Babblers (online book reviews)
www.bookbabblers.co.uk
Bookheads www.bookheads.org.uk
Books Unlimited
www.guardian.co.uk/books/booksforchildrenandteenagers
Children's Book Sequels
www.childrensbooksequels.co.uk
Petra Net (online book reviews)
www.peters-books.co.uk For members only
The Children's Laureate www.childrenslaureate.org.uk
The Children's Poetry Bookshelf
www.childrenspoetrybookshelf.co.uk
Cool Reads www.cool-reads.co.uk
Dyslexia www.Iamdyslexia.com
www.bdadyslexia.org.uk
Education City www.educationcity.com
Hobbycraft www.hobbycraft.co.uk
Learning Disabilities www.ldonline.org
Lovereading www.lovereading.co.uk/newgeneration
Mathletics www.mathletics.co.uk
Mrs Pancake http://mrspancake.com
My Home Library www.myhomelibrary.org
Newsround Press Pack www.bbc.co.uk/cbbc/presspack
The Poetry Society www.poetrysociety.org.uk
Primary Resources www.primaryresources.co.uk
The Reading Agency www.readingagency.org.uk
The Reading Club www.thereadingclub.co.uk
ReadPlus http://readplus.co.uk (subscription service)
School Libraries Advocacy
www.schoollibrariesadvocacy.org.uk
UK Children's Books www.ukchildrensbooks.co.uk
Word Shark/Number Shark www.wordshark.co.uk
Word pool Wordsearch Generator
www.wordpool.co.uk/resources/WSgenerator.php
Write Away www.writeaway.org.uk

Newspapers and Review Magazines

Books for keeps www.booksforkeeps.co.uk
First News www.firstnews.co.uk
The School Librarian (for members only)
www.sla.org.uk/school-librarian.php
TBK Mag www.peters-books.co.uk/tBkmag.htm
Times Educational Supplement www.tes.co.uk
Carousel www.carouselguide.co.uk
Writeaway www.writeaway.org.uk

Schemes

Booked Up www.bookedup.org.uk
Bookstart www.bookstart.org.uk
Boys Into Books 5-11 www.boysintobooks.co.uk

Boys Into Books 11-14
www.sla.org.uk/boys-into-books-overview.php
Summer Reading Challenge
www.summerreadingchallenge.org.uk

Training

CILIP Training
www.cilip.org.uk/training
SLA Training
www.sla.org.uk/training-courses.php
Your local School Library Service
www.sla.org.uk/links
Teacher Development Agency – TDA
www.tda.gov.uk

Events

Black History Month
www.black-history-month.co.uk
Children's Book Week
www.booktrust.org.uk/Campaigns/Childrens-Book-Week
CILIP Carnegie and Greenway Awards
carnegiegreenaway.org.uk
Costa Book Award www.costabookawards.com
International Children's Book Day www.ibby.org
National Non-Fiction Day http://nnfd.org
National Poetry Day www.nationalpoetryday.co.uk
National Storytelling Week
www.sfs.org.uk/national_storytelling_week
Roald Dahl Day www.roalddahlday.info
Summer Reading Challenge
www.readingagency.org.uk/children/summer-reading-challenge
The Man Booker Prize www.themanbookerprize.com
The Blue Peter Book Prize
www.bbc.co.uk/cbbc/bluepeter/getinvolved/bookclub
World Book Day www.worldbookday.com
World Storytelling Day
www.worldstorytellingday.webs.com

Publishers and Suppliers

Carel Press www.carelpress.co.uk
A to Z Supplies www.atozsupplies.co.uk
LFC www.lfccatalogue.co.uk
Micro Librarian Systems (Junior Librarian.net)
www.microlib.co.uk
Peters Bookseller/Kitshop www.peters-books.co.uk
Softlink www.softlink.co.uk

Library Guidelines

SLA Primary School Library Charter www.sla.org.uk
CILIP Primary School Guidelines ISBN 0 9543792 09

All of these links are also online at
www.carelpress.co.uk/offtheshelf
to save you having to type them.

CALENDAR OF KEY EVENTS

JAN

New Year

1st: Horses' Birthday
(official birthday of all
thoroughbred horses)

Costa Book Award

FEB

National Storytelling Week

2nd: World Wetlands Day

14th: Valentine's Day

MAR

1st: St David's Day

Crufts Dog Show

World Book Day

17th: St Patrick's Day

20th: World Storytelling Day

21st: World Poetry Day

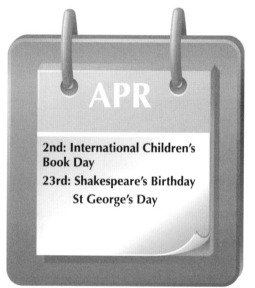

APR

2nd: International Children's
Book Day

23rd: Shakespeare's Birthday
       St George's Day

MAY

Local History Month

15th: International Day of
Families

Walk to School Week

Chelsea Flower Show

FA Cup Final

JUN

Recycling Week

5th: World Environment Day

8th: World Oceans Day

CILIP Carnegie & Kate
Greenaway Children's Book
Awards

Some dates change each year eg: Easter, Eid, Hanukkah, Guardian Children's Fiction Prize, Blue Peter Book Prize

CALENDAR OF KEY EVENTS

JUL

Summer Reading Challenge
4th: American Independence Day
14th: Bastille Day

AUG

1st Sunday: International Friendship Day

SEP

13th: Roald Dahl Day
26th: European Day of Languages

OCT

Black History Month
Children's Book Week
4th: World Animal Day
National Poetry Day
Man Booker Prize
16th: World Food Day
31st: Halloween

NOV

Children in Need
National Non-fiction Day
5th: Guy Fawkes Day
11th: Remembrance Day
30th: St Andrew's Day

DEC

11th: International Mountain Day
25th: Christmas

For a complete calender of key events, including those that change each year, see Successful Library Displays, Carel Press

PROMOTING THE LIBRARY

The aim of an effective school library is to promote reading and there are many essential ingredients to achieving this. Tricks of the trade – that have already been discussed – are important, but enthusiasm has to be maintained and supported throughout the year. It is essential to any library's success that it is promoted to its audience both within the walls: pupils, staff, and those outside the walls: parents.

A great way of inspiring both children and parents is by organising reading events.

READING EVENTS

During the year there are many different reading events that take place. I remember wondering how to plan my first event and where to begin. What I could have done with was an annual calendar of key events pertinent to primary schools, so I could look over the year and plan what events I was going to do. So when I decided to write this book, that was the first thing I wanted to create (see p24-25). I hope you find it as useful as I do.

As you will see there are many to choose from. When choosing an event, think about what you want to get out of the day and which event will suit your needs the best. Aims for the day may include:

- To enthuse pupils about reading and writing (Children's Book Week)
- To allow the children to celebrate a specific author (Roald Dahl Day), or genre of writing (National Poetry Day, National Non-Fiction Day)
- To support a curriculum topic
- To create publicity for the school
- To work as part of an event (Book Week)
- To promote your school's cultural diversity (Black History Month)

Once you have decided which events you are going to support, the next stage is to think how you are going to do it.

Basic

The easiest way to promote a book event is to create a display about it in the library and/or around the school. I always like to support our local Reading Festival, so I research any authors who are involved in the festival and create a display in the library that incorporates their books, including pictures or toys of characters from the stories. Then create a poster, or use one ready made and place them around school to advertise the event. These ideas can be adapted to fit any event and take very little time, space and budget to achieve.

Medium

Other events may require a more elaborate celebration, which requires more time and organisation, but no more budget!

OFF THE SHELF Carel Press www.carelpress.co.uk

Why not create a whole day of activities around a book event or even a whole week!

Many of you may be panicking at this thought and wondering where to start. Don't worry, as long as you plan ahead, anyone can do it. To make life even easier, I have put together a table to help plan activities for your day based on specific themes, (p59). The ideas are there for reference. Pick and choose the ones you like and feel free to adapt them to your needs. Make sure the activities you choose will make an impact and really create a buzz around reading. At the end of the day it's all about having fun with books! Alternatively, there are loads of great websites (p23) that will give you fantastic tips and ideas to help you organise your event.

If you find some ideas you like, great!

Choosing a theme

This is very important. Make sure you know what you want to achieve, it may be:

- To support the curriculum
- To promote a theme adopted by an annual event (Children's Book Week always has an annual theme)
- To promote a particular author
- To choose a theme that will create a buzz around books
- To promote reading within school

If the event involves the whole school, try to pick a theme that will appeal to all ages, or can be adapted for all. Remember to keep the focus on fun and the excitement that can be created from sharing fantastic stories!

Organising the event

Once you have chosen the theme, it's time to begin organising the event itself. The most important thing to do is give yourself plenty of time to plan.

Before the event:

Meet with the Literacy coordinator to get them on board to help organise the day. It's always good to share the load and have a partner to bounce ideas off. Talk through ideas for the day and put together a list that you can discuss with the Head.

- Meet with your Head and get the date of the event in the school diary, checking that nothing else is happening on the same date. Talk through your ideas and get her or his approval and support.
- Put your idea forward at the next staff meeting and gain the support of your colleagues.
- Meet with any other staff members involved in the day e.g. the school cook, school secretary etc.
- Contact your School Library Service – they may have advice or resources to help you make a success of the event.

Once you have established the activities begin to prepare and gather resources you will need:

Create eye-catching posters to advertise the event to children and parents (don't panic – event websites have great graphics and ideas to help, some even have ready made posters to use!) Make sure they include all the fun activities you have planned for the day. Place them in prominent positions around school and where parents will see them.

Create resources for competitions e.g. entry forms, quizzes, design sheets etc (if you run low on inspiration, look at event websites for fabulous resources). Remember to send them out before the event and to include a return date.

Create a timetable of events for the day, including timings for staff; the more information they have the more likely they are to join in the fun!

Write a letter to parents outlining the event and any activities that will require their attention e.g. dressing up theme, competitions etc. (This is when involving the school secretary will come in handy, as you will need help with distribution.)

> My favourite thing to do is to place about ten posters in a row on the fence the whole way up the school drive!

Check everybody involved has the date in their diaries.

Check websites for lesson plans and activities. Teachers always like support, the easier it is for them, the more likely they are to do it.

Print off and hand out any lesson ideas or resources for teaching staff if they require them.

Make sure teachers have access to any books supporting the event, so everybody can be prepared.

Contact the local press with details of the event.

Organise your own fancy dress outfit, if you don't join in why should anyone else!

On the day

Every event is different but here are a few guidelines to help the day run smoothly. The main thing to do is enjoy the day!

Make sure the camera has batteries in it so you can take pictures of the event.

Remind all staff involved of the details and timings of the day.

I like to visit all classes, first thing, and praise the children on their costumes and get them excited about the events of the day.

Be available all day to answer any queries and keep the day running smoothly.

Pick competition winners and arrange prizes. Be on hand during assembly to hand out competition prizes.

OFF THE SHELF Carel Press www.carelpress.co.uk

Meet with any local press organised and help arrange photographs. Remember to check parental consent of publication of pictures. Be aware of any children who cannot have photos taken.

Make sure teachers have all the resources they need to complete activities.

After the event

Ask the children and staff about their thoughts on the day (use them to improve future events).

Check on any follow-up work the children are doing. Create displays from any good work.

Look through the pictures of the day and create a display or book about the day, use quotes from children and staff to enliven it.

Cut out and keep any press clippings of the event.

Start planning for the next time!

Be ambitious!

If you want to really create a buzz, why not co-ordinate your event with an author visit.

AUTHOR VISITS

This is one of the most rewarding events that you can have. I know from experience that the children, and staff, get so involved and excited that as soon as it's over you want to arrange another one!

However, as exciting as it is, it is a costly event, requiring careful thought and planning. If you have the time and money, it is worth every penny. The following guidelines, I hope, will help you make the most of the author, illustrator or poet you invite to your school.

Why have an author? That's a question I have been asked by staff before and it's a valid one that is fundamental to the whole visit. Decide why you want an author to visit:

- To enthuse pupils about reading and writing
- To allow the children to meet their favourite author and have a chance to ask them questions
- To support a curriculum topic
- To create publicity for the school
- As part of an event (Book Week, Black History Month)
- To gain experience both personally or professionally for yourself

It is vital you understand your reason for the visit to make sure you are going to make the most of the opportunity.

> Putting on a fancy dress outfit is my favourite part and anyone who knows me will tell you that I am worse than the kids when it comes to dressing up!
> I have been: Miss Trunchbull, Mr Twit, a robot, Hagrid, a witch, a fairy godmother and an ogre to name just a few.

What sort of author do you want to invite?

When you have decided what your focus for the visit is going to be, the next stage is to research which author will tick all your boxes. Not only must the author meet your subject criteria, but you must also consider that not all authors are confident in visiting schools. On the other hand some authors can be truly inspirational. Things to consider are:

Does the author come recommended? (websites, library services, from other schools)

Many authors only write for specific age ranges, so make sure that the author you choose is suitable for your pupil age range.

What do you want the author to offer? Many authors offer a range of activities including readings, workshops and drama, whilst others are more traditional (readings and question/answer sessions).

How many children do you want the author to see during their visit? Does the author do small group workshops or large group presentations?

Most importantly – are the author's fees within your budget? Fees can vary, some authors offer deals where they visit for free, but ask for their books to be put on sale to the children.

Is the author available on the date you want them? Some famous authors can be booked up years in advance and many do not do school visits at all. Be aware of the timing of your event as even lesser known authors can be booked up in advance, especially around times of National Book Week or World Book Day. Plan ahead and be organised.

Information on the types of authors and illustrator visits can be found online.
For example:
www.societyofauthors.net
www.literacytrust.org.uk
www.artscape.org.uk

Preparation

When you have decided on the author you would like, the next stage is to contact them. Most authors have agents, but it is always better to contact them direct to avoid any errors in arrangements. I always think contacting them in writing, via email, is a good start (include a contact number/address) and arrange a convenient time to telephone them to discuss your requirements. These may include:

- The date of the visit
- The age of the children they will be talking to
- The size of the group
- The number and timing of the session(s)
- The length of session you require
- The venue, check it meets the author's needs
- Whether they need any technical equipment
- Refreshment arrangements and any dietary needs

- The agreed fee, including travel expenses and VAT if appropriate, and details of payment
- The titles of the book(s) the author will be discussing
- Whether there will be a book sale or signing
- Travel arrangements

Once you have agreed the above details, always follow the phone call up with a letter confirming all the details. At this point make sure you also give them any details they may need:

- School contact name (include a back up name in case of illness)
- School address, phone number and email (include a clear map, if necessary).
- Confirm arrival time and any collection details, if necessary.
- If you are collecting the author, include the mobile number of the person picking them up.

Before the visit

- Try to start the promotion early as it gives you time to create a real buzz of excitement about it.
- Make sure that all staff and children know about the visit.
- Create a display, in prominent position(s) around the school, to promote it. It may be worth contacting the author or publisher to see if they have any promotional material to help.
- Let class teachers have a copy of the author's book to read to the children.
- Create a display of the author's books in the Library, using any photos, pictures or posters you may have.
- Get the teachers to discuss the visit; what will happen, how to behave, possible questions they want to ask the author.
- Write a letter to parents/carers telling them about the visit – including details of book sales etc.
- Make sure your camera has batteries in it and check that the author is happy for photos to be taken.
- Contact the local press with details of the visit. Remember to check parental consent of publication of pictures. Be aware of any children who cannot have photos taken.

The Visit

Every visit is quite different, but I hope these guidelines will help the day go as smoothly as possible. But most importantly ENJOY IT!

- Remind all staff involved of the details of the event.
- If you are collecting the author, be on time.
- Be ready to meet and greet the author on their arrival (speak to the school receptionist, or secretary and make sure they are aware of the author's arrival. A welcome drink is always appreciated!)
- Make sure refreshments are available for the author during their visit.
- Escort the author to the venue.
- Check that all the author's technical requirements are in place and working.
- Make sure that staff and children arrive on time for the event.

- Introduce the author to the audience.
- Be around to guide the author through the whole time they are visiting, don't leave them to fend for themselves in the staff room or dining hall at lunch!
- If you are having a book sale, check it is organised and running smoothly.
- Very important – make sure payment/invoice has been organised and is ready for the author.
- Thank the author.
- Make sure all return journey arrangements are met (lift to station etc).

After the visit

- Ask the children to write thank you letters to the author and choose a selection to send.
- Ask the children about their thoughts on the visit.
- Check on any follow-up work the children are doing.
- Make sure all payments are made on time.

I have read a lot of information about organising author visits and have come to realise that there are some common pitfalls that everyone should be aware of:

- NEVER leave the author alone with the children, they are not covered by public liability insurance.
- All teachers of children in the audience should be present (and other teachers/ teaching assistants if available). They should be fully engaged in the presentation and NOT marking books!
- If you have any children with special needs or behavioural problems, let the author know.
- Make sure any press are invited before or after the presentation, you don't want them arriving in the middle.

AND FINALLY ... ENJOY!

P.S. Then you can get on with arranging the next one!

BOOK WEEK

Every Book Week I create a four page A4 booklet about the event, usually with a picture and title on the front, a timetable of events happening during the week in the middle and interesting information about why we are doing the event on the back. This is sent out to all parents to promote the week to them and to advertise what is happening.

During one book week, we made a KS1 and KS2 book. Each key stage was given a genre (fairy tale – KS1, adventure – KS2). In KS1 Reception wrote the beginning, Year 1 the middle and Year 2 the end. In KS2 Year 3 wrote the beginning, Year 4 the dilemma, Year 5 the resolution and Year 6 the ending.

The book was passed to each year group every day until it was completed. On Friday we made the stories into big A3 books and they were read out during assembly. The children were very proud to be authors. We photocopied the books to A5 size and gave one to each child to keep.

ENGAGING PARENTS

As a Primary Librarian you are in a unique position to meet with parents face to face on a daily basis, a captive audience! When encouraging children to read, the biggest advocates you can have are parents. The first influences in children's reading are their parents; bedtime stories, nursery rhymes etc. If you can gain the support and enthusiasm of parents, then you have a better chance of capturing the child. Research has shown that families are key to engraining positive reading attitudes in children, and those children who view their parents as reading role models are more likely to be enthusiastic readers themselves.

Including parents in reading activities at school will help inspire parents to come into school, particularly those parents who might otherwise be reluctant. There are many simple ways to get parents involved in reading, it doesn't matter how simple it is, just engaging them in any way is a positive. Here are my favourite activities, I hope you try them as they are very rewarding, not just personally but more importantly, for the children and their parents.

Family Libraries

Why not open your library to pupils' families? This sounds like hard work, but I promise you once you get it up and running, it's actually great fun. We began this a couple of years ago, after requests from parents who were struggling to get to their local library or those who just wanted to get some advice about what books to choose for their children.

Before launch

The first thing to do is to sort out the practicalities of running a family library.

- Who will run it? (either yourself or a willing member of staff)
- When will you run it? At Hill West we chose to open on a Wednesday after school from 3.30pm until 4.30 pm, but you can decide the day, length and time that suits you best.
- Will you make library cards for parents for them to keep or store them at school?
- Will your library stock be sufficient to accommodate extra borrowers?
- What allowance of books will you give families? (Our limit was six books per family, for a maximum of four weeks)

Once you have decided it's an idea you want to pursue, the next questions are will parents want to use it and when to launch it?

It's a good idea to launch at the start of a school year, when parents are enthusiastic about the coming year and new parents arrive in Reception. So spend time during the summer term gauging interest from parents about the idea.

Write a letter outlining the idea, with a tear off slip for parents to fill in if they are interested in using the library. It should also request information about user name, name of child/children, class name(s). Make sure all new Reception parents for the next school year receive one too.

Create library cards (parents and children love to have a card!) Ours is laminated and includes the school logo.

Before the end of term, send out the new library cards with a covering letter, the starting date, time and staff in charge.

If you really want to create a buzz around the launch, why not make the first session even more fun by holding a craft session, where parents and children can design their own laminated bookmark or have a short story session where the children listen to a story while the parents browse. This looks really impressive, but takes no time or money to plan. If you decide to do this, don't forget to advertise it!

Week of the launch

Make sure you have the book or books you will need as well as all the resources. If you are holding a craft session then check bookmarks, pens, pencils, laminator and sheets.

Send out a letter to parents to remind them of the launch date and time, ask any parents interested in joining to send in their details on a tear off slip.

Make sure your library is looking at its best!

If you have a management system make sure it is working – there's nothing worse than having parents standing there holding books and not being able to issue them!

Plan timings for any craft activities or reading sessions, making sure there will be enough time to complete tasks.

Launch

- Have all your resources and everything else set up and ready
- Be there to greet parents as they arrive
- Put music on or an audio book to create the right atmosphere
- Follow timings of activities promptly
- Be available for parents to ask questions. This is the perfect opportunity for parents to quiz you on reading with their children. Be confident, be informative and be supportive.
- Give parents a 15 minute warning before the end of the session, otherwise you'll be there all night!
- Enjoy yourself as much as the children and parents – your enthusiasm for reading will rub off on them!

After launch

Hopefully the launch will have gone so well that you'll have more parents enquiring about joining. Keep a track of the number of borrowers, you may need to increase stock if the idea becomes very successful!

It's also important to keep up to date with overdue books as it is easy to lose track with an increase in loans.

Story and craft sessions

If you feel confident and have the extra time, why not maintain interest in your Library Club by holding a story or craft session every term or half term. Make sure you get the parents involved with working with their children. It is so rewarding for all involved. Some ideas:

Theme	Reading	Craft
Festivals: Christmas Divali Chinese New Year Easter Halloween	Stories linked to festival	Christmas cards Tree decorations Colouring character pictures Make a lantern Easter cards Make an Easter basket Make masks Design a pumpkin lantern
Book Event	Stories linked to theme or author	See 'Planning a themed event' p59
World Events Olympic Games World Cup	Biographies of athletes Stories about sports Stories set in other countries Stories from other countries Football stories Player biographies	Make flags of countries Olympic Flag Colour in flags Design a football shirt
Launch of film based on a book	Read extracts of the book	Themed colouring sheets

These are just brief ideas, let your imagination run wild and create your own ideas.

PARENT STORY BAG WORKSHOPS

Primary schools are in a unique and powerful position to work closely with parents. We can support, advise and use parents to inspire their children to read. I have had many opportunities to talk to parents and the overriding desire they have is to be involved in their child's learning, to learn skills to read effectively with their child and to work with them in the school environment. These conversations were the inspiration for the workshops. At Hill West our thought was to hold these workshops for Reception parents each year, but they could be adapted for any year group, although I have found non fiction texts work better in KS2. Our thinking was to capture new parents at the beginning of their journey through education and by catching them early, we could help them learn the skills to read effectively, as well as inspire them to create a reading ethos in their home.

'The story bag session really brought the books to life and gave me a great opportunity to work with my child and to learn how to read effectively with them.'
Parent

As the name suggests this idea is about inviting parents into school to work with their children to make story bags, which in turn can be used as a learning tool in the classroom.

You may be asking, what is a story bag? It's simply a sack or, as I like to use, a pillow case, which contains a story book along with related craft ideas, games, learning tools and other fun activities.

Why would you want to make a story bag? With the ever increasing concerns regarding children's listening and speaking skills and the worrying decline in an interest in reading, story bags are perfectly placed to offer a wonderful range of resources. They will stimulate talk and careful listening, whilst helping develop a life-long love of books and stories. Imagine the fun of not only reading about the characters in the story but also making masks and puppets of the characters, playing related games, wearing costumes, and much more.

So how do you make a story bag? Begin with the bag, it doesn't have to be fancy, just large enough to fit the contents into. Decorate the outside with the story title and pictures to match the story you have chosen. I like to use felt, which I stick on using PVA glue, but you could use fabric pens/paints or, if you are handy with a needle (unlike me!) you could sew straight onto the bag. Make it bright and colourful, the more attractive, the more inviting it will be.

What goes into a story bag?

I try to keep things simple. There is a basic formula for the contents:
- Book
- A cd or tape of the story (top tip: buy it if you have the budget or record yourself reading it for a cheaper option)
- Finger puppet, masks or related toys to retell or act out the story.
- Homemade jigsaws of pictures from the story.
- A simple related game e.g. pairs, snap or bingo.

For older children:
- Create board games linked to the book
- Make a wordsearch or crossword on the computer
- Design their own fun worksheets on the computer

Whatever you decide to include, make sure they are activities that can be made by parents and their children. Items like colouring pages and worksheets can be added at a later date, for use within class.

This doesn't have to be a huge amount of work for one person because it involves teaching staff who can help you to plan, organise and run this event.

Planning a workshop

Before:
Again the most important thing to do is give yourself plenty of time to plan and organise any event like this. I usually give myself 3-4 weeks.

Top tip: If this is your first time organising a workshop, start small, I did. It's much better to have a trial session with a small group of parents, also you are not having to make as many resources. I ran my first workshop with 12 parents from one class and then repeated the session the following week with 12 parents from the other class.

Now to the organisation:
Choose which year group you are going to run the workshop with. As I explained, I chose Reception, it's a great opportunity to catch the parents at the beginning of their child's schooling and they are usually very keen! However, you could choose any year group and adapt.

Meet with the year group teaching staff to discuss:
- the date (the beginning of the year is always a good time or the beginning of a new term)
- size of group (whole class or small group) this will affect the rest of the planning
- topic that the session will support
- how many story bags you will be making (if a small group, one, if the whole class you may want to make more)
- story to base story bag around
- Time of session
- Length of workshop
- Location (based on the group size) – check availability
- What you want to get out of the workshop.

The last point is the most important, as it will dictate the organisation of the whole workshop. Every workshop emphasis may be different depending on your parents and their needs:
- To teach parents how to read effectively with their children
- To encourage reluctant parents into school
- To include parents in their child's learning by sharing the curriculum with them

- To encourage parents to work with their children
- To inspire parents to read with their children and teach them the importance and benefits of reading in a child's education

Construct a letter, with staff, inviting parents to the workshop (see template on the Off the Shelf website).

This should include:
- Aims of the workshop (as above)
- What they will be doing and how it supports the curriculum
- The date and time of the session
- Who can attend (parent, grandparent, friend, aunt, uncle etc) and the benefits for the child of working with an adult
- A tear off slip to book a place (with a cut off date for replies)
- If it's for a small group, make sure you let them know there are limited spaces and it will be based on a first come, first served basis

Once you have done the initial planning and letter, it's time for the fun stuff, organising the activities!

Make sure, the whole way through, that you work with the year group teaching staff. They are experts in their children and what they need, they know the curriculum and how to support it. The workshop will be more successful if they get involved.

With staff

Choose a book to base a story bag on. Make sure it's an inspiring book that you all like and one that supports your objectives.

Write a list of learning objectives you want the activities to support.

Look through the book together and discuss activities for the parents and children to make (they must match the learning objectives).

Write up a list of activities then allocate everyone an activity to organise resources for. It is important to include an instruction sheet.

The Week Before

Collate the names of the adults attending. If you are holding a whole class session, make sure all the children have an adult to work with. You may need to draft in help, so all the children have a good experience.

Discuss with the year group team the logistics of the session:
- who will lead the session (giving a brief introduction)
- timings of session
- who will read the story
- who is supporting each activity
- the logistics of the activities e.g. will each parent have a pack of activities to work through (small group) or a table for each activity and parents move around the tables (whole class)?
- Will parents do all the activities or just a few each?

Check that all the activity resources have been made and write a list of anything else you will need for each one i.e. scissors, glue, pencils, pens, laminating sheets etc. Begin to gather them.

- Confirm the location for the workshop is booked.
- Organise tea, coffee and biscuits for the parents.
- Write the introduction including your aims, how the session will run, timings, description of each activity.
- Make the bags to hold the activities (parents will love to see them, so make them nice, bright and colourful)
- Make evaluation sheets for the parents to fill out at the end of the workshop (see template on page 63).

The night before
- Remind parents about the workshop.
- Set out all the tables.
- Set out all the resources, making sure anything electrical e.g. laminator, is working.
- Put batteries in the camera.

On the day
- Before the workshop talk to the children about what they are going to do and how you expect them to behave.
- Check that everyone understands their roles.
- Set out the tea/coffee and turn the water urn on!
- Greet the adults as they arrive.
- Once seated, bring the children in to join their adult.
- Introduce the session (aims, what's happening, timings)
- Read the story to the children (you may want them seated on the floor for this), modelling to the parents how to read effectively (questioning, get them to retell the story etc)
- Introduce the activities and briefly explain what to do for each.
- Answer any questions.
- Set them off. I love to wander around for some of the workshop and take photos of the children working with the adults. The concentration and enjoyment on their faces is priceless (and that's just the adults!)
- Give them a 5 minute warning of when you will have a break.
- The break is a great opportunity to talk to parents and answer any questions relating to reading and books. I always find it easier for someone to take the children outside for a short play during the break.
- Again give them a warning 5 minutes before the end of the session.
- At the end of the session, take the children back to class promptly to avoid any tears (with little ones).
- Give the children a date that the bags will be ready for them to use (generate some excitement)
- If there are any activities that adults have not completed, give them the opportunity to take them home to complete and return to school.
- Close down the session and ask for an evaluation sheet to be completed by all adults and collect them in.

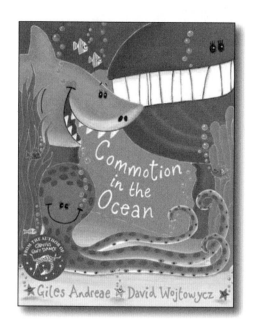

After the workshop

Try to create the story bags as quickly as possible and use them in class – otherwise the excitement about them will wane and parents will ask if they are being used.

Look through the evaluation forms and discuss feedback for future workshops.

I love to create a display, either in the Library or in the classroom, showing how much fun the workshop was. The children love to see photos of themselves working.

One very successful story bag we made was *Commotion in the Ocean*, by Giles Andreae and David Wojtowycz, chosen to support the Literacy topic of rhyming. Below are the activities we created. They will give you a good idea of the games you can make, please feel free to adapt as you wish.

Book: Commotion in the Ocean

Masks	Line drawings of characters' faces, crayons, laminating sheets, scissors, lollipop sticks, masking tape or Sellotape.
Snap game	Line drawings of the main characters, blank squares of paper for snap cards, laminating sheets & scissors.
Animal Bingo	Bingo grid: grid on paper, sheet with a selection of colour pictures of animals in the story, scissors, laminating sheets. Bingo cards: blank squares of paper, pictures of animals, laminating sheets and scissors.
Jigsaws	Several colour copies (A4) of scenes from the book, laminating sheets, scissors, pencils to draw jigsaw piece shapes on back, envelopes to store the jigsaws in.
Reading match activity (colour names)	Sheet with colour names: pink, blue, green, orange, yellow, purple, white, black (which represent the colours of the sea creatures in the story) in block lettering so they can be coloured in by the children x2. Pencil crayons, scissors, laminating sheets.
Instruction sheet	Instructions for the parents on how to complete each resource.
Copy of the book	

Other great books to create story bags around are:

KS1

The Hungry Caterpillar, Eric Carle (healthy eating, lifecycles)

The Bad Tempered Ladybird, Eric Carle (telling the time)

Mrs Rainbow/Madame Arc-en-Ciel, Neil Griffiths (introduce colours, seasons, room names in French)

Farmer Duck, Martin Waddell and Helen Oxenbury (teamwork)

The Little Red Hen, Michael Foreman (co-operation and sharing)

Little Moon, Stuart and Nicola Clark (space)

Fairytales (Jack and the Beanstalk, Goldilocks and the Three Bears, The Gingerbread Man)

Nursery Rhymes (individual ones)

Each Peach, Pear, Plum, Janet Ahlberg and Allan Ahlberg (Nursery rhymes, rhyming)

Old Lady Who Swallowed a Fly, Pam Adams (sequencing, counting, memory skills)

KS2

Just match a topic area to a good quality, high interest non fiction book e.g. Egyptians (We're Sailing Down the Nile)

Once you have found an activity that appeals to you it's time to start promoting!

SUMMER READING CHALLENGE

A great way to promote reading and link to your local library is the Summer Reading Challenge. Organised by the Reading Agency, this is the biggest national reading initiative. Its aim is to inspire children, aged 4-11, to read during the long summer holidays. Research has shown that taking part can help prevent the 'summer holiday dip' in reading motivation as well as boost attendance at local libraries. Sounds good? – then read on to find out how you can get involved.

Summer Reading Challenge, the Reading Agency. Photo: Dave Warren

- Each year has a different theme with a dedicated website packed with games and activities to keep the children engaged and motivated www.summerreadingchallenge.org.uk
- Children sign up for it at their local library and receive a free starter pack.
- The Challenge invites them to read six library books of their choice during the holidays.
- The children then collect rewards and incentives along the way to encourage them to complete their challenge.
- Library staff are on hand to advise the children and there are activities to encourage families into the library throughout the holidays.
- It's a great event to promote during summer term through displays, invitations to families to take part or classroom-based activities to generate interest.

For more information contact your local library!

THE SCHOOL LIBRARY ASSOCIATION

'They are the encouraging voice on the end of the phone, the friendly face at a training course or the supportive word in an email'

The SLA believes that every child is entitled to a well resourced school library run by trained, knowledgeable and enthusiastic staff, with support from good Schools Library Services. The SLA provides training courses around the country, an annual weekend course, and a varied range of publications as well as an advice service for members. *The School Librarian* journal contains articles, reviews of books and ICT resources as well as news and information. The website (www.sla.org.uk) is a mine of information. The SLA works with many other organisations to improve the lot of libraries in the UK and beyond.

I can't tell you what an honour it was to accept my award from such a prestigious organisation as the SLA. To have your work acknowledged by an organisation of people with such a depth of experience was, to say the least, humbling. In my experience they work tirelessly to support all Library practitioners to create the most effective libraries possible. Whatever your experience or knowledge, they are the encouraging voice on the end of the phone, the friendly face at a training course or the supportive word in an email. Without their hard work and dedication, many children would be unable to access the library resources they deserve. Long may they continue!

SUPPORTING THE CURRICULUM

The Library is not only a place to inspire reading, but also a place of learning. The Library should be at the heart of any school, supporting both teachers and children to fully access the whole curriculum.

LOCAL LIBRARY

Partnerships can be one of the ways to create excellent school libraries, especially a partnership with your local public library. Schools should work closely with their local library to arrange class visits, reading activities, homework support and help for children to develop information literacy and research skills. When we visit our local public library, pupils are treated to a morning or afternoon session with professional librarians teaching them information skills tailored to their age group. These sessions are a valuable tool, helping the children to learn how to use a library effectively.

Discuss with your local library what sort of lesson you would like: a specific subject or general information literacy. They are always happy to tailor lessons to your needs in a professional and effective way. If you don't have a local library near you, then a trip could be organised or why not invite the librarians to your school instead?

CHOOSING BOOKS

Choosing the most effective books for the Library should be collaborative; including the children, staff, outside organisations, websites, book awards and so on.

Ask the teachers

Teachers are an amazing and, more importantly, free source of information. Like the children, asking their advice makes them feel valued and a part of the Library family. Their expertise comes from: their experience, their understanding of the children in their class and their knowledge of what the children should be reading.

Choosing fiction can be tricky but I have always found choosing non fiction even harder. To make the Library into a true information centre, the non fiction section must reflect what is being taught in the classroom. It is here that the teacher's knowledge comes into its own. In my first year as Librarian, I looked through all the curriculum notes for each year group and wrote down all the topic areas covered by each year group. Easy, so I thought. What I hadn't fully realised was the array of texts there are on any given subject. Did I want a book on India that covered its geography, culture or people? What I have learned since then is to find out from the teachers not only the curriculum topics they are covering but more specifically the sub areas of that topic. To do this with each individual would take too much time, so I created a Library Book Purchasing sheet (template p58) that I give the teachers at the beginning of the year on which they write topic titles for that year and specific details of subject areas where the Library is lacking material. This information is invaluable and makes choosing books much easier and more effective.

Book reviews and awards

If you have more time, there are a vast number of journals and websites that provide you with vital information about children's literature including book reviews, award winners, top tens to name but a few. You will find a list of some of them on p23.

There are also several children's book awards every year such as Blue Peter Book Award, Carnegie Award, Kate Greenaway Award and the Roald Dahl Funny Book Prize. These awards may be judged by authors, literary experts or children themselves. Whoever judges them, they are a tremendous source of inspiration when choosing books. Award winning books can also be made into a quick and easy display, showing the book, author photo, award logo and other books by the same author. The children always love to read books that have won awards, especially those chosen by other children.

School Library Service (SLS)

The SLS has been my greatest source of support since taking over the Library. Their knowledge and expertise in children's literature is invaluable to both the experienced and inexperienced librarian. The SLS are part of local councils and wherever you are in the country there will be either an SLS in your local authority or one in a neighbouring authority you can subscribe to.

Their primary role is to give support and advice to librarians about all aspects of running a Library; planning and design, organising your Library, advisory service, including training, purchase facilities and IT support. However, my favourite resource is their book loaning service. For a nominal fee, they will loan boxes of books to schools. You can choose how many boxes you require and the content by topic, author, theme, fiction, non fiction, genre – it is really up to you. There are many different ways to use this service depending on your requirements and budget:

- each year group can be supplied with a box every term that relates to their topic(s),
- single box loans to the library relating to specific events (e.g. Black History month)
- or a box of books for a specific group of children (books for boys).

They are a great way to supplement your library stock and you have the peace of mind that the choice of books has been made by experts.

RESEARCH

The ability to use books for research is a fundamental skill that children should be learning from a young age. Certainly by the time they start secondary school, they will be expected to have the basic skills to research subjects, sift out the important information and use it effectively. A comment I get a lot from secondary school teachers and librarians is that Year 7 children always look lost when asked to do a research project and rely heavily on the guidance of the librarian. Wouldn't it be fantastic if we could arm them with these skills at Primary School! Well we can. Many of these we have already discussed in previous chapters.

As more and more schools change the way they plan to a more topic based approach, the more the library is going to be relied upon as a source of information. Whatever system your school uses, most non foundation subjects are topic based.

The easiest way to introduce research in both KS1 and KS2 is to provide classes with books specific to the topics being taught. These could be books you have gathered together yourself from library stock, or topic boxes loaned from your local School Library Service. Whichever source you use, the books will allow teachers to give the children opportunities to browse through books for themselves. In KS1 research can be done in an informal, organic way, but in KS2 actual research lessons can be planned, giving opportunities for research skills to be taught in a more formal format.

If you have a library with adequate stock and space to accommodate a whole class, research lessons can be held in the library itself. At Hill West, many teachers introduce a new topic by visiting the library. They plan a guided session, which allows the children to research the new topic independently. We are lucky that our facilities let us use both the internet and books to research, but using just books is great too. The children love the freedom and it gives them real ownership of their work. Teachers who have used the library in this way tell me that the quality of the children's work and their enthusiasm for the topic is much higher when they work like this.

If you are a dedicated librarian or have more release time, you could lead research sessions yourself. Your expertise and knowledge of the resources in the library are invaluable (and, naturally, teachers like to hand over the reins to others sometimes!) Try to make it a fun lesson as many children have a negative view of research, which will reflect in their work.

Library Sweep Game

Before any research activities can take place, children must be familiar with the basics of the Dewey system. A great game to play from Reception to Year 6 is an adaptation of 'Supermarket Sweep'! This is like a treasure hunt. You make each clue lead to a certain subject, a specific topic, Dewey number or area of the Library. There are examples of clues on page 46. Obviously you can tailor your clues to your pupils. You should laminate cards with the clues on, then hide them in either a specific book or on a shelf. You need a starter whistle or bell and an egg timer.

When the children come in divide them into groups so there are the same number of groups as clues. Begin by reading the first clue to the first group. Let them work out the clue and then start them off with the whistle or bell (don't forget to turn over the timer), they have until it runs out to find the clue (with older children you may want to include thinking time in the 3 minutes to make it harder). If they find the clue in the allotted time they win a prize (younger children like to win a laminated star, older children prefer housepoints!), if they don't the next group gets the opportunity to find it for extra points! When the clue is found, it is read out to the next group and so on until all the clues are found. The group with the most stars or points, wins (although you usually find it's a draw, so everyone wins!)

The activity can last for as long as you want; I think it works best as a quick warm up activity to begin every lesson in the library, or as a library induction lesson. I actually did this activity with staff as an induction lesson and they had more fun than the children! Mind you they weren't as good at it as the children!

There are many different books which contain great research activities but my favourites ones are 'Murder in the Library', and Web versus Books which are in *Great Library Ideas* (Carel Press) which can be adapted to any subject.

OVER TO YOU...

Well, my writing journey is now complete and what a journey it has been. At the beginning my aim was to produce a simple step by step handbook for creating an inspiring library, I truly hope I have achieved that. My other wish was that I would give you confidence and support to get out there and have a go yourself. Never be afraid to try something new and different, think 'off the shelf' and, most importantly, have fun with it. Good luck and, as Dr Seuss once said: "Unless someone like you cares a whole awful lot, nothing is going to get better. It's not."

I would love to know how you get on, so drop me a line and tell me your stories!
lucy@carelpress.co.uk

Clues for Library Sweep game

They are the top predator in the ocean and can be great white, lemon, reef, tiger or nurse.

Answer: Shark

Neil Armstrong landed there in 1969.

Answer: Moon

This musical instrument is in the woodwind family and rhymes with root.

Answer: Flute

Read about the lives of real people here.

Answer: Biographies or Dewey 920

In which country would you find the Acropolis?

Answer: Greece

Which Tudor king had six wives?

Answer: Henry VIII

This organ pumps blood around the body.

Answer: Heart

They came in longboats from Scandinavia.

Answer: Vikings

You'll find writing that rhymes here.

Answer: Poetry books

Who painted the Mona Lisa?

Answer: Leonardo da Vinci

This sport involves bouncing a ball and slam-dunking it into a net.

Answer: Basketball

How to find your books!

004   ICT

200s   Religion

300s   People, Society

500-549 Science

550-599 Nature

600s   Technology

700s   Art, Music, Sport

800s   Poems

900s   Geography, History

Pupil Librarian Photo Frames

OFF THE SHELF www.carelpress.co.uk   You can download this resource in colour

Reading
Certificate

presented to

_____

INVITATION

You are invited to the library to join me in the Boys into Books Club

On

At

Look forward to seeing you there!

RSVP

INVITATION

You are invited to the library to join me in the Boys into Books Club

On

At

Look forward to seeing you there!

RSVP

INVITATION

You are invited to the library to join me in the Boys into Books Club

On

At

Look forward to seeing you there!

RSVP

INVITATION

You are invited to the library to join me in the Boys into Books Club

On

At

Look forward to seeing you there!

RSVP

Larger size colour template available online www.carelpress.co.uk/offtheshelf

Boys into Books

Boys into Books

Boys into Books

Boys into Books

Books on the web

Top Readers

Stars for top readers

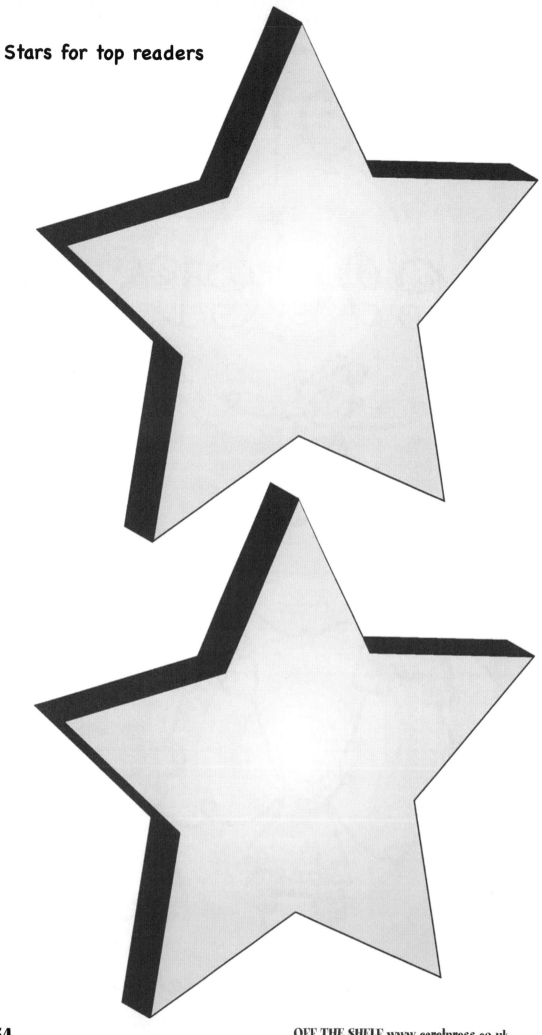

OFF THE SHELF www.carelpress.co.uk
You can download this resource in colour

TOP 10
Non-Fiction

1
2
3
4
5
6
7
8
9
10

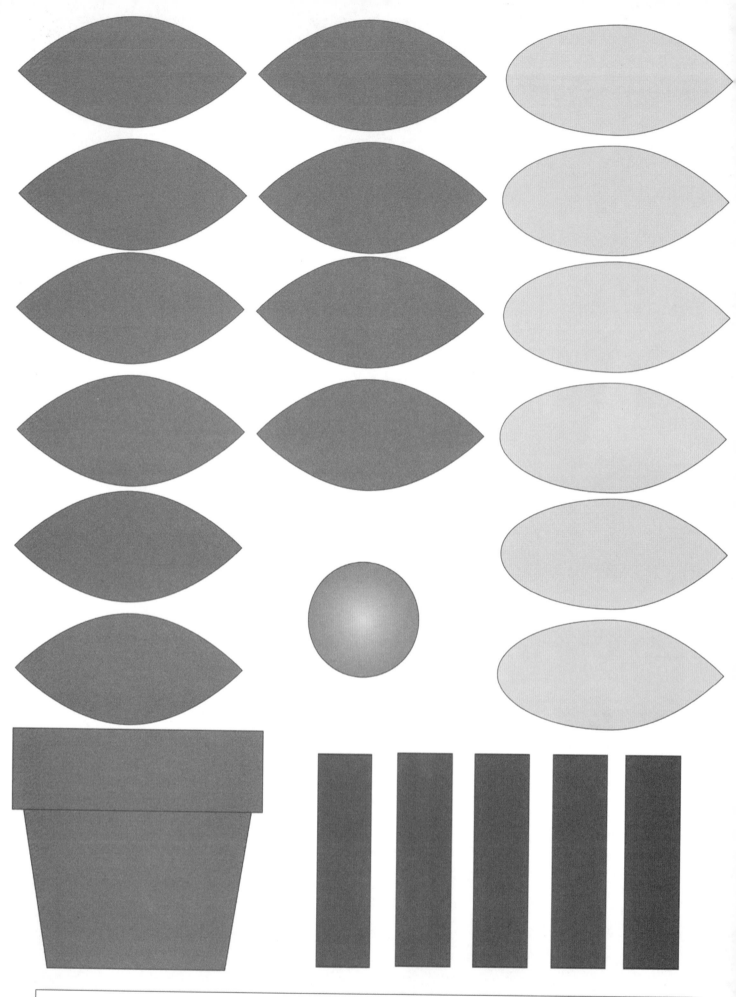

Top fiction books sunflower template, see p9,
larger size colour templates available online www.carelpress.co.uk/offtheshelf

TOP 10 Authors

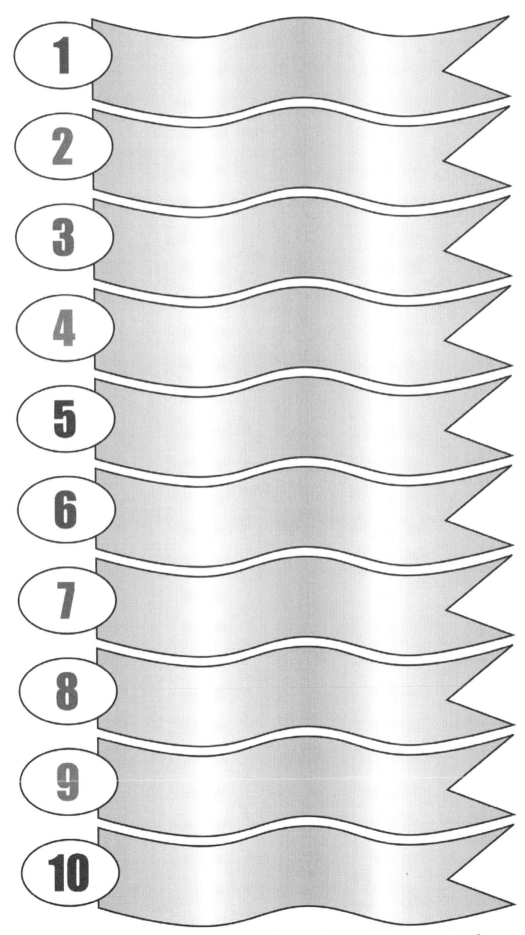

1

2

3

4

5

6

7

8

9

10

Library Book Purchasing

Areas not covered by Library stock

Name:

Year Group: Date:

Subject: Topic Title:

Area of study:

Subject: Topic Title:

Area of study:

Planning a themed event

Theme	Costume ideas	Competition	Writing/Reading activities	Other activities
Bedtime Stories	Pyjamas Fairytale characters	Design PJ's for favourite book character and label design	KS2 write and make their own bedtime story and read to KS1 children. KS1 bring in their favourite bedtime story and share with class.	Ask for lunch to be an all day breakfast
Roald Dahl Day	Favourite Roald Dahl character	Best costume. Design own Willy Wonka sweet and describe it.	Children invent their own marvellous medicine and explain what it does. Write your own revolting rhyme based on a fairytale.	Rename lunch menu after Roald Dahl food e.g. snozzcumbers
Creative Curriculum/ Topic	Costumes based on topic chosen e.g. Space (Aliens) Electricity (robots) Habitats (Tribal costume) Water (undersea creatures)	Create bookmark around your topic Best costume	Read stories based on topic. Write a book review about stories shared.	A costume parade
Poetry/Nursery Rhymes	Nursery Rhyme character	(KS2) Create a picture based on a descriptive poem. (KS1) Draw picture of favourite nursery rhyme character Best costume	Write acrostic poems based on a chosen word e.g. POETRY Write a diary as if you are a nursery rhyme character.	All classes learn a choral poem and perform it to rest of school or film it to show. Create music to accompany it. Poetry X Factor. Groups or individuals perform poems and a winner is chosen. Have a Teddy Bear's Picnic on the field.
Stories from other cultures (each year group given a different country)	National dress or country's national flag colours e.g. Brazil (yellow and green)	Name the flags quiz. Country landmarks quiz Design flag for made up country and explain it	Choose stories from chosen country and share them. Write your own. Create travel brochures for the chosen country.(KS2) Pack a suitcase with all the things you need to visit chosen country (KS1)	Lunch menu reflects countries around the world. Children learn a song/poem from chosen country and perform them. Make and try food from chosen country. Research about chosen country and have a quiz.
Magic/Myths/Legends	Wizards/witches Harry Potter characters	Create your own spell/potion and explain what it does	Create your own mythical creature and describe it. Write a story about it. Create your own recipe for a potion. Write a poem about your potion.	Name lunch menu after food from Harry Potter or potion ingredients e.g. tadpole jelly, lizard tongue soup. Have broomstick races on the field Rename school houses for the day. Collect housepoints and see who wins the house cup.
Animals	Dress up as an animal	Create your own animal, name it and describe what it eats and where it lives.	Choose a book with an animal theme e.g. Polar Bear, Polar Bear, What Do You Hear? by Eric Carle. Write your own version using patterned language. Make it into a book and share it with younger pupils. Using chosen book research one of the animals and write a report on it. Create a class book.	Make animal headdresses and have your own Rio Carnival parade.
Fairytales	Fairytale characters	Design a costume for a fairytale character.	Design an invitation to Prince Charming's Ball. Write a diary as one of the characters in a fairytale. Write a newspaper report about an event in a story	Hold a Ball in the hall. Send invites to each class. Create character masks and perform the story.
General ideas	Book character	Book character quiz	Write a whole school story. Choose a genre and each year group writes a different part of the story. Put it together and make it into a book to share in assembly. Could be done in each Key Stage. Write a newspaper article about an event in a story.	During the day, if staff see pupils reading, they give them a raffle ticket. At the end of the day, tickets are drawn and winners receive a prize.

Tell me what you want to read

Borrow a book today!

Return your books here

STORY BAG WORKSHOP EVALUATION

Name

Year Group   Date

Were the activities clearly explained
and easy to follow?

Did you and your child enjoy the
activities?

What did you and your child gain
from the workshop?

What would you change?

Book Review

Book review written by _____

Date _____

Book title _____

Author _____

What the book is about _____

_____

_____

_____

_____

_____

What I liked best _____

_____

_____

My favourite character is _____

because _____

Who should read this book? _____

A question I would like to ask the author or a character _____

_____

Rating: ☆ ☆ ☆ ☆ ☆ ☆ ☆ ☆ ☆ ☆

OFF THE SHELF Carel Press www.carelpress.co.uk